DESSERTS-

A delicious learning, baking, and eating experience!

Sylvia Lee

Published by:

Green Tree Publishing LLC
PO Box 205
Birmingham, MI 48012-0205

ISBN # 0-9742452-0-8

Library of Congress # 2003094004

"We've had the privilege of serving a variety of Sylvia Lee's cakes at THE LARK RESTAURANT, and every one of them was delicious. She obviously has a perfect palate, which is essential to create a great cuisine. I'm getting hungry just remembering her Chocolate Framboise Torte and Lemon Crunch Roll."

Jim Lark, **THE LARK RESTAURANT**
West Bloomfield, MI

"The art of pastry is the art of love, and no one displays more art and passion than Sylvia Lee with her beautiful and tasteful creations. I have enjoyed her scrumptious delights for over 20 years and still have sweet memories of my favorite Stained Glass Torte."

John Jonna, **MERCHANTS FINE WINE**
Dearborn, MI
Royal Oak, MI
Grosse Pointe Woods, MI

"For many years our catering company enjoyed the wonderful and unique baked confections from Sylvia Lee's bakery. To this day we have been unable to find anything that can compare to Sylvia's Lemon Crunch Cake, or her Raspberry Cheesecake with the fabulous nut crust, as well as so many other cakes and tortes by Sylvia."

Mary Rembelski & Kathleen O'Neill
CANAPÉ CART, Inc
Royal Oak, MI

"Sylvia Lee cakes were of the highest quality and were very popular."

Gary Cashman, manager, **QUARTON MARKET**
Birmingham, MI

"The carrot cake was so delicious it should be called 24K Cake because it was so rich. The chocolate Kirschtorte left you craving even more. Just the thought of the Raspberry Cheesecake makes my mouth water. One of my fondest memories is sharing the Chocolate Framboise Torte on my Wedding Anniversary."

Alice Phelps Currier, owner,
LONG LAKE MARKET
Bloomfield Hills, MI

"Sylvia's cakes were the first ones eaten from the sweet table. They are delicious!"

Fadi Abdulnour, general manager,
SOUTHFIELD MANOR
Southfield, MI

Notes

Many thanks are in order…

I thank my husband Larry for his deep intelligence and sound judgment that have been my wisest council. Throughout our 43 years of marriage, Larry has advised, encouraged, and supported all of my dreams and projects.

My children, Howard and Vi, Sandy and Sherwyn, Margo and Ethan, Karen and Tony have individually and collectively helped me with computer techniques, legal issues, graphics, public relations, tasting parties, constructive criticism, editing, suggestions, suggestions, and more suggestions!

My parents, Harry and Pearl, who inspired me with their wonderful parties, where my mother baked all of her luscious Viennese tortes - many of which you'll find in this book.

My friends, who gave their time enthusiastically to test recipes and proofread, and forgave my unavailability when I was too busy to socialize.

My late friend, Audrey Kron, who affectionately urged, encouraged, and inspired me to write this book.

Last but not least, I thank the many people whose repeated requests for my recipes told me that there is an audience craving these desserts.

I dedicate this book to my dear grandchildren who unconditionally and enthusiastically love whatever I give to them – as I love whatever they give to me.

Sylvia

Notes

Table of Contents

****PLEASE READ BEFORE EACH BAKING ENDEAVOR!!!!!!!**

Photography by Norman Weiss

Introduction

All roads lead to the kitchen! This has been my mantra, as my love for baking and experimenting with recipes has been pure pleasure for me – and I find myself wanting to be in the kitchen. No matter what the interest and configuration of a family, everyone walks in and out of the kitchen constantly. We love to eat, we're enticed by good smells, and the kitchen tends to be a "comfort" zone. Indeed a good place to be!

Years ago I baked all the cakes for the social functions of my family and friends. I loved the baking, and it gave me great satisfaction that they enjoyed the desserts of my labor. When the demand for my desserts outgrew my ability to provide them from my home kitchen, it was time to open my own pastry shop. Providing homemade delicious cakes was a wonderful experience for me, my family, and for my grateful customers.

I've written the recipes in this book in a way that is very easy to follow. The recipes are written in chronological order with ingredients clearly identified and steps spelled out simply, yet with sufficient detail to assure success. I truly feel that if a person respects good food and loves to prepare it, that person will be a competent and successful baker.

One of the most treasured compliments I got when I had my shop was when a young man said, "Sylvia, don't take this wrong, but your cakes remind me of the great stuff my grandma used to make." I assured him that that was the highest compliment he could give to me. That compliment summarizes the taste that these cakes evoke – a caring person in the kitchen who wants only to serve the tastiest and best.

You, dear reader, have the extra pleasure and gratification of giving your newly baked offerings to those you love.

I hope you and yours enjoy,

Sylvia

Notes

Rules to Bake by…

1. **READ THESE RULES BEFORE EACH BAKING ENDEAVOR!**

2. The speeds of mixing are "slow", "medium" and "fast"- nothing fancy - just what you have at home - a standard 4 quart mixer or even a hand-held electric mixer will work.

3. When adding ingredients, follow these recipes in chronological order. You will use fewer utensils and make less of a mess.

4. No matter what time or temperature the recipe indicates, you must check for doneness because all ovens vary. Do this by inserting a metal skewer or wooden toothpick into the cake. When you pull it straight out, if no wet crumbs stick, the cake is done. THIS DOES NOT APPLY TO CHEESE CAKES!

5. All extracts - vanilla, almond, etc., are PURE - no imitation anything. PURE is best and leaves no aftertaste.

6. When beating, mixing, stirring, etc.- always stop a few times to scrape the sides and bottom of bowl with your rubber spatula.

7. When using nuts, toast them for about 2 - 4 minutes in 350° oven - or toaster oven. Toasting enhances the flavor.

8. Rotate pans once in oven during baking time.

9. Whip whites and whipping cream until peaks form that do not fall down - then stop!

10. When recipe calls for butter, use SWEET UNSALTED butter.

11. Always use LARGE eggs.

12. Oven should always be PREHEATED.

13. Oil should be CORN or VEGETABLE - not olive oil.

14. Use ALL PURPOSE flour and do not sift it.

15. Unless otherwise stated, sugar is GRANULATED.

16. Unless otherwise stated, chocolate chips are SEMI SWEET.

17. Unless otherwise stated, cocoa is UNSWEETENED and UNSIFTED.

18. Unless otherwise stated, ENJOY baking and SHARING your good bounty!

Notes

Helpful Hints

1. Measure all ingredients and have them ready to go before you even turn on the mixer. This bit of preparation makes for a smoother baking experience, and eliminates frustration.

2. When using butter, margarine, or cream cheese, always take out of wrapper when cold. This is much easier, less sticky, and less messy. However, since it blends better and faster when at room temperature, put it in bowl you will be using and cover with plastic wrap or plate for 1-3 hours prior to using.

3. To grease pans - take paper towel with a big glob of Crisco, or similar vegetable shortening, and spread generously around sides and bottom of all inner surfaces. In my experience, sprays, butter, or margarine do not work as well.

4. Use this tip for grating lemons, limes, or oranges: First cut fruit in half and squeeze out the juice. Grate ½ fruit at a time by putting 4 fingers into the hollow of the fruit and putting your thumb on the outside skin. Then grate it against the grater while you rotate the fruit half. Fingers will be protected, and it will be easy!

   I also recommend using the pulp that you have squeezed - why not - it just helps to intensify the flavor. This is in addition to the measured amount of citrus juice. Naturally, remove and discard the seeds!

5. Cakes usually unmold better when they are lukewarm - about 15 minutes after removal from the oven. The cooler they get, the more likely they are to stick to the sides and bottom of the pan.

6. To unmold pans - place a flat platter on top of lukewarm cake and invert. Sometimes after inverting, covering the bottom of the pan with a hot damp towel for a few minutes will make the cake come out more easily.

7. To freeze, put cake uncovered in freezer for about 2-3 hours. When no longer sticky, slide cake into large zippered plastic bag and continue to freeze and store.

8. If a piece of eggshell falls into the food, use a bigger piece of shell to reach in and scoop it out. Seems as if "shell attracts shell".

9. For apple cakes, use "baking" apples. Every region and season offers different types. Ask your produce manager to recommend the right one. As a "default", Jonathan, Empire, or Macintosh work well.

10. When melting chocolate in double boiler, heat on low and don't let any water splash in. Water hardens chocolate and makes it unusable.

Notes

Trims and Fancy Touches

There are two reasons for finishing our cakes with some sort of fancy touch. First and foremost you want an elegant presentation. Second, you need cover-ups to hide some of your "sins". If there is a slight unevenness, if a patch stuck to the pan, if the glaze is not glossy in parts, if the frosting doesn't look fluffy, etc., etc., etc., - that's where a chocolate leaf, meringue quill, even confectioners sugar dusting come in to do their duty.

We use just a few trims. These are very versatile and can be used on a variety of cakes. The "leaves" and "quills" may seem daunting to you at first, but they are so easy once you have done a few – so stay with it!

In my pastry shop, everyone would fight for who got to make the leaves for the week. There is something very soothing and pleasant about sitting on a stool at a kitchen counter replicating with your own hands the wonders of nature. You think I sound corny, but just try it and you'll soon be humming "Autumn Leaves" while creating a compost pile of leaves - both in dark and white chocolate.

The trims we will use are:

1. Chocolate flakes - dark or white
2. Chocolate leaves - dark or white
3. Chocolate shards - dark, white, or butterscotch
4. Confectioners sugar and cocoa dust
5. Confectioners sugar over a stencil
6. Fruit leather flowers
7. Ground chocolate or vanilla cookies
8. Ground nuts
9. Meringue "quills" – dark or white
10. Silk, plastic, or nontoxic real flowers
11. Stained glass
12. Stunning strawberries

Chocolate Flakes

The food processor does all the work!

Use grating blade and put **chocolate candy bars, chunks, kisses,** or any **white** or **dark chocolate** through tube on top. Hold plunger down to push chocolate towards grater.

Empty your contents often into airtight plastic or glass container. Do not pack down too closely. Don't touch with your hands because the warmth will melt the delicate flakes. Store in a cool, dark cupboard. Refrigerator and freezer have too much moisture and moisture causes the chocolate to turn whitish.

When ready to use, take spoon and gently sprinkle sides and tops of frosted cake - as generously as pleases your eye.

Chocolate Leaves

Go to the florist (a day or so before you plan to start on this project) and buy about 2 branches of lemon leaves (Salal). Select branches that have as many uniformly sized leaves as possible. Break leaves off branches and wipe with a damp cloth and let dry.

Melt in small double boiler: **8 oz. chocolate chips - white** or **semi sweet**

With a small spatula, preferably the half-sided one, spread thin veneer of melted chocolate over VEINED side of leaf. Spread thickly enough so that green doesn't show through - just a little thicker than the real leaf. The technique you use can be either to hold the leaf lightly between thumb and pointer finger, letting rest of leaf lay atop middle finger as you spread with the other hand; or, put leaf on counter and spread there.

Put covered leaves on a flat cookie sheet and refrigerate for about ½ hr. This short time in refrigerator won't harm the color.

Peel chocolate off gently by holding stem and slightly bending it down as you lift chocolate off with other hand. Try not to touch it too much with your (warm) hands.

If you are careful, you will be able to use leaves again and work in relays until you have used up all of the chocolate.

Store leaves loosely lined up in a tight sealed container that lets in NO moisture. A cool dark cupboard is best. Refrigerator and freezer let in too much moisture and moisture causes the chocolate to turn whitish.

Make leaves out of dark, milk, and white chocolate and keep them on hand for lots of beautiful touches.

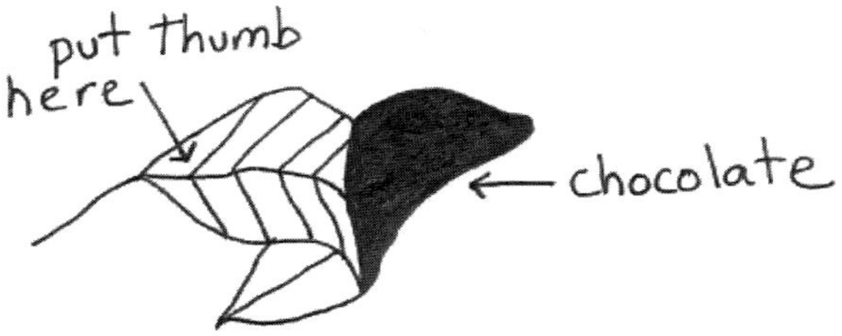

Chocolate Shards

Melt in double boiler: **1-12 oz. bag chocolate chips** OR **white chocolate chips** OR **butterscotch chips**

Spread a large rectangle of the melted chocolate, using a spatula, on a marble or formica surface. The spread should be about ¼" thick.

Let cool to room temperature.

With paint scraper (about 2"-3" size) or small metal spatula, scrape away from you pushing scraper on bottom of chocolate spread - thereby creating broken hard pieces in random sizes - i.e. “shards”.

Store in dry, sealed container. Perfect for using on sides of cakes - covers uneven glaze, uneven size, and adds great taste and texture.

Confectioners Sugar and Cocoa Dust

Combine equal amounts of confectioners sugar and unsweetened cocoa into a small strainer with tiny holes.

Hold strainer with one hand while tapping its side with other hand. The sugar and cocoa will lightly rain down. Cover the whole surface of the cake, tipping cake slightly to get to the sides.

Confectioners Sugar Over Stencil

Buy, or make out of cardboard or parchment paper, a stencil of a snowflake, heart, initials, etc., etc., etc.

Lay stencil lightly on top of cake. The cake could be frosted with glaze, jam, chocolate shards, cookie crumbs, or whatever you want.

Put confectioners sugar into a small strainer with tiny holes.

Hold strainer about 4" above cake with one hand, while tapping sides of strainer with the other hand - as you rotate around all the surfaces.

CAREFULLY - with upward motion, remove stencil and see your instant “drama”.
If you used red jam, the effect is white on red. If you used chocolate shards or crumbs, the effect is white on black. Dramatic!

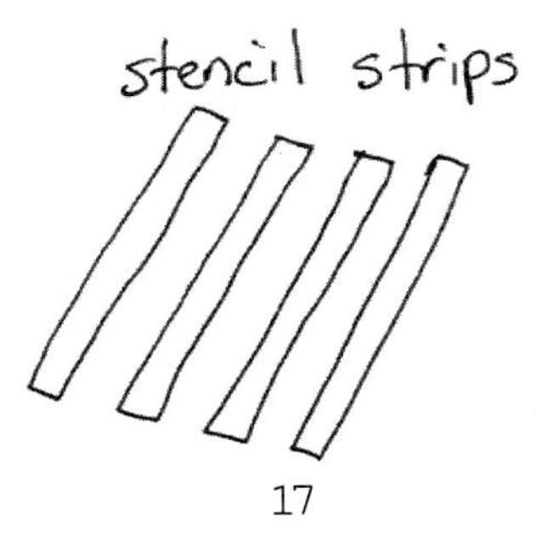

Fruit Leather Flowers

Buy the **fruit leather** that comes in rolls by the foot. They're usually found in the children's snack section or by the candies in the grocery store. Buy a nice variety of flavors (that means a variety of colors)!

Now, lay one roll at a time out flat on a cutting board. Using small flower shaped petit-fours cutters with sharp bottoms, press down firmly on "leather" and cut as many as you can.

When ready to use, spread flowers all over top and sides of cake. Take a small tube of colored gel in a different color and put a dot in the middle of each flower. This adds to the realism! You will get the effect of a generous, abundant bouquet. This look can be really charming and refreshing. Best of all, only you and I will know if it's covering up any flaws.

These can also be done ahead of time and stored in the cupboard in a tightly closed plastic bag or container. Don't refrigerate - they will get too hard.

Ground Chocolate or Vanilla Cookies

Put **sandwich cookies**, **vanilla wafers**, or **chocolate wafers** in food processor. Process quickly until you get crumbs. This is a lovely way to cover a cake whose frosting tastes better than it looks - a dense cover of tiny crumbs adorned with one fresh flower on top makes a dramatic and elegant, and best of all, easy presentation.

Ground Nuts

Grind in processor any size you want (just be careful it doesn't grind into a paste), or buy ready ground. Press into top and sides of frosted cake. Carefully tip cake to get sides covered. Sometimes it's easier to spread your hand wide and hold cake on bare palm and tip with one hand while pressing nuts into sides with your other hand.

Meringue Quills

Preheat oven to 250°

In mixing bowl, whip on medium	**3 egg whites**
Slowly add:	**¼ t cream of tartar** **6 T sugar**

Continue to whip on "high" until stiff.

Pile into pastry bag with #10 tip. This is a tip with a small round hole - about ¼" across.

Make continuous lines across length of: cookie sheet lined with parchment paper, ungreased

Bake 4 hours or until no longer sticky.

When cool, break into about 2" sticks. These get studded into the frosting all over in a haphazard array - to resemble a porcupine.

Store in a tight sealed container - in a dry room. Remember moisture makes meringue sticky, so do not refrigerate or freeze.

To make dark quills - follow above recipe, but into meringue add: **1/3 C dark cocoa**, sifted.
Stir gently with spatula until blended. Continue with recipe as above.

Silk, Plastic, or Nontoxic Flowers

These are always elegant - if they are not too big and overwhelming. Just one flower placed either in center or off to one side of cake OR with stem under cake and bud peeking from outer ridge looks very pretty.

Stained Glass

This beautiful cake covering can be placed on top of any layer cake that has been frosted. The fondant base used here is very sweet and usually people just peel it off of their individual slices before eating. That's fine because by that time they've ooh-ed and aah-ed enough over the presentation!
This is not as hard as it looks!

Combine in large bowl: **4 C confectioners sugar**
½ C white corn syrup
2 egg whites

Knead by hand until mixture is smooth.
Make a fat patty.
Sprinkle counter generously with: **corn starch**
Roll out a large enough circle to drape over cake.
Fold circle into quarters, lift, and drape over cold frosted cake.
SO FAR YOU DID JUST WHAT YOU DO TO GET A PIE CRUST - only with fondant.

Make a little cone out of parchment paper and tape it together. This resembles a tiny ice cream cone, dunce cap, or child's party hat.

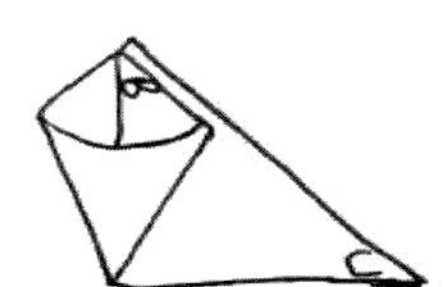

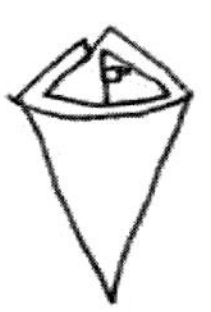
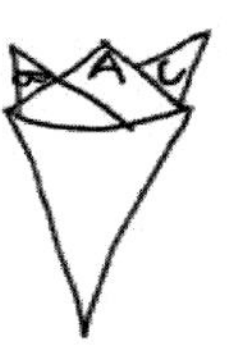

Into cone pour: **¼ C chocolate chips**, melted and slightly cooled.

Clip a tiny hole off tip (where ice cream usually drips) of cone.
Now, scroll around with the chocolate - filled cone to make a random design that has lots of circles and ovals contained in it:

When chocolate scroll is dry, fill in circles and ovals with: **colored gel in tubes**
To even the bottom edges of fondant-covered cake, make chocolate or colored gel border OR place pretty fern leaves around outer perimeter, thus hiding uneven or ragged edges.

Stained Glass Torte

Stunning Strawberries

This is a very dramatic way to finish a plain, ordinary chocolate cake. Cinderella couldn't have wished for a prettier transformation!

Into any frosted chocolate cake push in firmly to completely cover the top surface: **pretty strawberries of even size**

Glaze each strawberry with: **melted apple jelly**

Surround sides of cake with: **chocolate wafers** (available in 9 oz. pkg.)

Push wafers firmly into frosting.

Place on pretty silver or crystal platter and prepare to take many compliments.

Blueberry Cheesecake

Rocky Road Chocolate Cheesecake

The ultimate of riches: nutty, marshmallowy, crunchy rocky road candy covers a well deserving chocolate cheese batter. This cake "wants" to be frozen - it unmolds better, slices better, tastes better, and frees you of last minute dessert worries!

Preheat oven to 275°

Crust:

In medium saucepan, melt: **4 T butter**

Add: **1 C chocolate wafer cookies,** finely ground (½ of a 9 oz. package.)

Press evenly into bottom of: 10" spring form pan, greased

Cheese filling:

In small pan, melt
1 T butter
1 C chocolate chips
1/3 C whipping cream

In mixing bowl, beat on "medium":
3 – 8 oz. packages cream cheese
1¼ C sugar

When fluffy, add and beat on "low" until blended:
6 eggs
½ C whipping cream
½ t vanilla
above chocolate mixture, slightly cooled

Pour mixture into: above wafer lined pan

Put spring form pan in large roasting pan that is 1/3 filled with water.

Bake 2½ to 3 hours. Cake should have a slight jiggle in center.

Cool at room temperature for 2 hours. Then take off only spring form side and put cake in freezer for 2 hours.

Rocky Road Frosting:

Combine in medium pan over "low" heat:
½ stick butter
½ C whipping cream
½ C cocoa, sifted
½ C confectioners sugar, sifted

Stir for 5 minutes until smooth and glossy.

At this point, you have made a most delicious glaze that would do any cake proud. However, for the "rocky" you must add:

¼ C **chopped nuts** - your choice
¼ C **miniature marshmallows**
¼ C **crunchy cereal,** any kind
¼ C **raisins**

Presentation:

When Rocky Road glaze cools, spread on top of cake that was in freezer for 2 hours. Return cake to freezer and leave overnight uncovered and unwrapped.

The next day you will unmold cake from spring form bottom using this trick:

Put frozen cake on burner on high. Count to fifteen quickly. Turn off heat. Slide metal spatula between cake and pan bottom and lift cake into freezer-proof plastic bag.

Return to freezer, and when you want to serve it, remove and put on serving platter about 2 hours before serving time. This can be at room temperature. If longer, put in refrigerator.

Now here comes the bad news - this cake does not slice well at a buffet table where the cutter doesn't have time to put the knife in hot water between slices. My solution is that you slice this cake when it is FROZEN. Cut 14 – 18 pie-shaped slices and leave in a circle touching each other - in other words, still in the round.

Serves 14 - 18

Rocky Road Chocolate Cheesecake

Chocolate Cakes and Tortes

Chocolate Kirschtorte

A single layered rich, dense amalgamation of semi sweet chocolate, cherry preserves, and cherry liqueur. Almost like chocolate quicksand - for chocolate lovers only!

Preheat oven to 375°

Batter:

In small double boiler, melt:
1 C chocolate chips
6 T Kirsch (cherry liqueur)
1 stick and **2 T butter**

When melted, remove from heat and cool to lukewarm.

In mixer, beat at "medium" until frothy:
4 eggs
¾ C sugar

Turn off mixer and add:
chocolate batter mixture
¼ C flour

Turn mixer to "low" and mix for 5 seconds - (just until blended).

Pour into: 9" pan, well greased
Bake 25 minutes

Let cool until lukewarm (about 15 minutes) and then invert onto working platter.

Filling:

Scoop out soft insides of cake, leaving a 1" rim around the circumference. Make sure that when you scoop you leave a layer of sufficient thickness on the bottom so that it doesn't break.

Combine "scoopings" with:
4 T cherry preserves
2 t Kirsch

Refill cake with this mixture - making sure to have a smooth surface.
Refrigerate or freeze for a few hours so that cake feels sturdy enough to frost.

Frosting:
In medium saucepan, melt:
5 T butter

Turn off heat and add slowly, while stirring:
1 C heavy cream
1 C sifted cocoa
1½ C confectioners sugar, sifted

Turn heat on to "low" and stir slowly for 5 minutes.
Turn off heat and add:
1 t vanilla

Cool slightly and pour over cake.

DO NOT use any tools to smooth the top surface - it will dull the sheen. Instead just keep tilting the cake (on the platter or on your hand) until the top is covered with glaze. I know that you're thinking that this is a pain to do – please believe me that it is SO DELICIOUS that it's worth every minute of stirring and "tilting".

You may, however, use a spatula for spreading the sides because you will be covering the sides with chocolate leaves.

Presentation:

Put cake on pretty platter with extra room around sides.
Place chocolate leaves slightly overlapping around sides of cake. They will stick to the still-wet frosting. They basically make a garland around the sides of the cake.

If the top surface is smooth - leave well enough alone. If the surface has a few flaws - put 3 chocolate leaves on top and place a tiny silk, plastic, or real (nontoxic) flower in the middle - just as in nature!

Serves 10-12 nature lovers

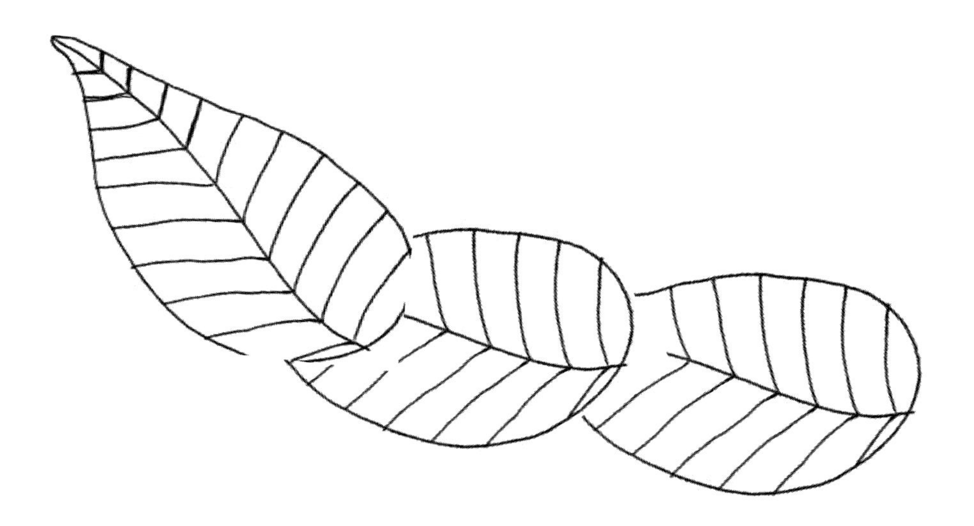

Chocolate Kirschtorte

Chocolate Log

The great "outdoors" comes "indoors" and deserves a hearty welcome! Perfect to use as a Yule log. This cake batter will become your best friend - as you will also use it for the Mousse Bar and Pinwheel Torte - two other winners!

Preheat oven to 350°

Batter:

In small double boiler, melt: **1¼ C chocolate chips**

In mixing bowl, beat until thick:
6 egg yolks
½ C sugar

Turning mixer to "low", add:
above chocolate, cooled
2 T espresso, cold

In separate bowl, whip on "high" until stiff: **6 egg whites**

With spatula, by hand, gently fold whites into chocolate until just blended - about 15 strokes.

Pour into:
12" x 16" jelly roll pan:
grease, cover with parchment paper
grease paper

Bake 15-20 minutes

When cool, put clean kitchen towel on top of cake and carefully flip pan over so that towel is on the bottom. The towel should be big enough to overlap on all sides so that you can fold it over the pan as you flip. Gently peel parchment paper off and you're ready to fill:

Filling:

In mixing bowl, combine and whip until peaks form:
1 C whipping cream
½ C confectioners sugar
1 t vanilla

Spread whipped cream evenly on cake (that is still on towel).

Using towel to push from wide side, roll into a jellyroll and wrap up both ends with towel to keep firm. You will have a long roll.

Place towel-wrapped roll (sausage look) in freezer. If using soon, freeze for 2 hours until shape firms up, then remove towel and place roll on serving platter.

If freezing for up to a month, leave in towel 4-6 hours, then remove towel and replace with foil wrapping to store.

Presentation # I

Cut 1" slice off both ends of roll at about a 45° angle.
Place one slice on top of log and the other at the side of the log touching as closely as possible. These will resemble knots that are on logs.
Using a small strainer, sprinkle over entire log a mixture of:

2 T cocoa powder
1 T confectioners sugar

Using the tines of a fork, run squiggly lines down length of log all the way around top and sides - to resemble a piece of bark.

If making a Yule log. Follow same instructions, but surround log on platter with evergreen branches. Then sprinkle a little confectioners sugar over branches.

Serves 8 - 10

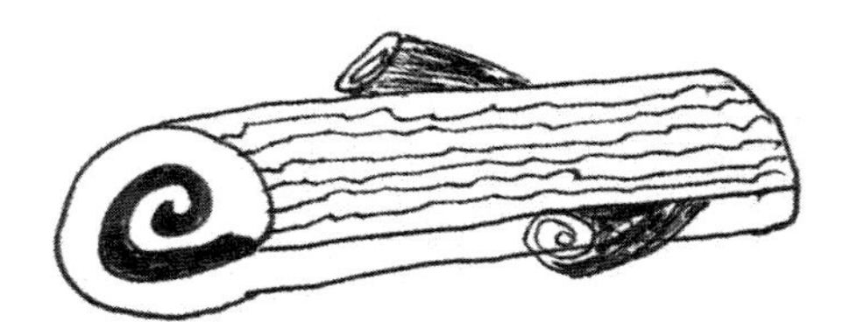

Presentation # II:

Chocolate Mousse Bar

This variation of the above cake is delicious and easy.

Instead of rolling, you will cut the cake in three even pieces. You may cut along the width or the length, depending on the size of your serving platter. You will have either a long, narrow roll, or a short, wide roll. Both work well and the size flexibility enables you to use whatever platter you have without having to buy a new one. See how I save you money?

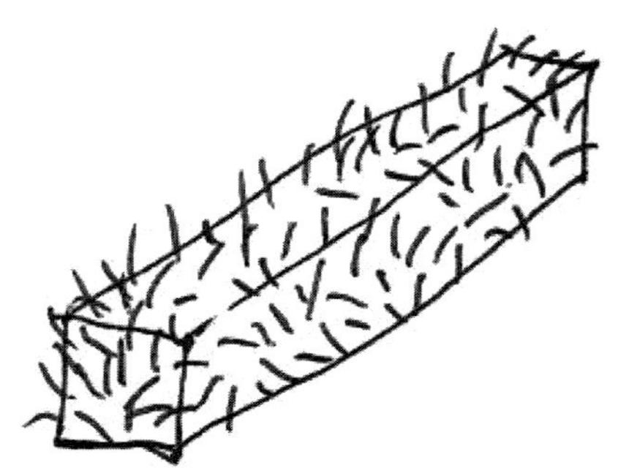

Now stack the three layers using the chocolate frosting from Devilsfood Cake (p.43)

Stud the entire top and sides with chocolate meringue quills. (p.18).

Chocolate Mousse Bar

Chocolate Pinwheel Torte

Next to my family - this is my pride and joy! Everyone loves it. Use it for wedding cakes (where people will tell you that it's the first wedding cake they actually ate.) Use it for Passover cakes, as it has no flour. Use it for shower cakes, as it is light and not too filling. Use it for Bar/Bat Mitzvah cakes as children and adults love it - and on and on and on.

The drama occurs when you slice this cake because of the unique way it is made which makes the layers vertical - each slice is black and white and black and white standing up. To see it is to believe it!

Batter:

Follow recipe of the Chocolate Log

Lift baked cake out of pan by holding the parchment sides.

Cover cake with whipped cream following the filling recipe from the Chocolate Log. (p.37)

Creating the Pinwheel:

1. Using a sharp knife, make four strips evenly spaced running the long length of the cake.

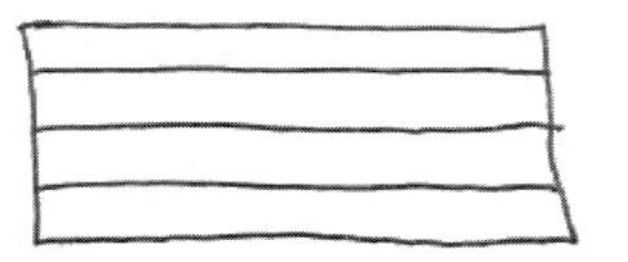

2. Slide a knife under one edge piece and when loosened from parchment, roll into tiny jellyroll with frosting on the inside. Place in center of large serving platter, cut side down.

3. Loosen second strip from parchment and arrange around roll on platter with frosting side on inside, connecting new strip with end of previous strip. You have now used two strips.

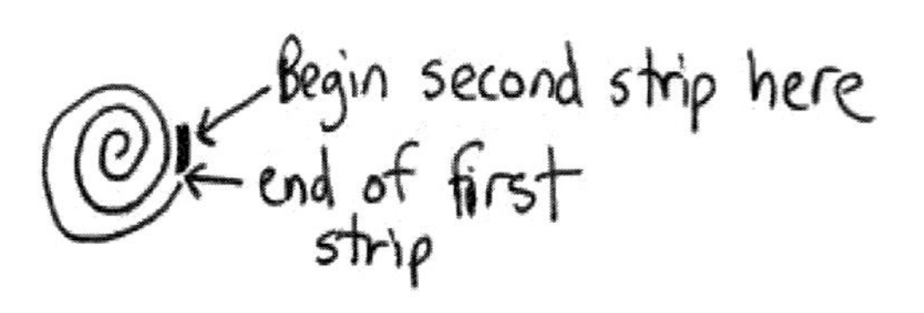

4. Continue forming pinwheel, connecting each new strip with end of previous strip.

As you look down at this, you see alternate swirls of chocolate and whipped cream. This is good.

Frosting:

Whip until peaks form: **1 C whipping cream**
3 T confectioners sugar
1 t vanilla

Presentation:

Completely cover top and sides of cake with frosting. Cake may not be a perfect circle because of the strips, so compensate by using frosting as "filler".

Over frosting top press in: **1 - 2 C chocolate shards** (p.17)

Place cardboard strips evenly on top of cake leaving same width space between each strip.

Heavily sprinkle **confectioners sugar** over entire top.

Quickly lift cardboard strips (stencils) and you will have a black and white striped top.

Surround the sides with: **40 - 50 cylindrical shaped cookies** standing as if making a fence around cake - either plain or dipped*

OR: **35 - 45 chocolate wafer sticks**

OR: **1 - 2 C chocolate shards**

When you slice this cake you MUST make pie shaped slices to get the full drama of the vertical slices.

Serves 8

*To Dip:
Melt in double boiler: **2 C chocolate chips**

Holding cookies one at a time with tongs, dip into warm chocolate covering all surfaces. Give a little shake to remove excess chocolate.

Place on: cookie sheet lined with parchment paper, ungreased

Chocolate Pinwheel Torte

Devilsfood Cake

"Listen my children, and you shall eat: Dense chocolate, rich chocolate, a chocolate treat!" This is a perfect blend of rich batter and crunchy mousse. Perfect for birthday cakes.

Batter:

Preheat oven to 350°

Combine in bowl:

2 C flour
2/3 C cocoa
2 t instant coffee crystals
1¼ t baking soda
¼ t baking powder

Turn mixer on to "slow" and add:

3 eggs
1¼ C sugar
1 C mayonnaise
1 C strong cold coffee

When ingredients are well blended, pour into: 2 - 8" pans - well greased

Bake 30 to 35 minutes.

Unmold when lukewarm.

Frosting:

Melt in microwave or double boiler: **1 C chocolate chips**
Set aside to cool

In mixer, whip at high speed: **1 C whipping cream**

When peaks form, pour above chocolate into whipped cream and stir gently with spatula. Most of the chocolate will blend, but some will harden and form those wonderful little pieces of "crunch" that only chocolate can do!

Presentation:
Fill between layers with chocolate cream. Frost sides and top of cake using a spatula and "light" hand to produce a fluffy look.

Serves 8-10

Framboise Torte

"If chocolate be the food of love, eat on." Woo them with this heart-shaped, chocolate, framboise-laced inspiration. This is an appreciated gift for Valentines Day - or any time you're feeling affectionate.

Preheat oven to 350°

Batter:

Melt in double boiler on "low" heat, in medium saucepan:	**1 C chocolate chips** **2 T raspberry liqueur** **1 T raspberry jam**
With hand held mixer, beat in slowly:	**1 stick** and **1 T butter** **½ C sugar**
Remove from heat and continue to beat, adding:	**½ C flour** **3 egg yolks**
In other mixer, whip until peaks form:	**3 egg whites**
Slowly pour in:	**pinch of salt** **dash cream of tartar** **1/3 C sugar**

Pour whites into cooled chocolate pan and with hand held mixer, blend for 10 - 15 seconds.

Pour into:	8" heart shaped pan, greased (or round pan)

Bake 35 minutes.

Unmold when lukewarm.

Frosting:

In medium saucepan melt:	**5 T butter**
Turn off heat and add:	**¾ C whipping cream** **1 C cocoa,** sifted **1½ C confectioners sugar,** sifted

Turn heat to "low" and stir until smooth - about 5 minutes.

Cool slightly and add:	**2 T raspberry liqueur**

Chocolate Singles

Caramel Brownies

The Thesaurus doesn't have enough adjectives to describe this marvel!

Preheat oven to 350°

In double boiler combine and melt:	**14 oz. package caramels** **1/3 C evaporated milk**
In mixing bowl, combine and blend, just until incorporated:	**mix for chocolate cake -** previous recipe (p.47) **1½ sticks butter,** melted **1/3 C evaporated milk**
Add, and blend 5 seconds:	**1 C chopped nuts** - your choice
Press ½ mixture into bottom of:	9" x 13" baking pan, greased
Bake 10 min.	
Remove from oven and pour over top:	**melted caramel mixture**
Sprinkle on top:	**½ C chocolate chips**
On top on this, pinch pieces, flatten, and spread evenly:	remaining above batter*

Bake 25 - 30 minutes.

Cut into bars or slices when still lukewarm. Lift off with metal spatula before it gets too cool and sticks to pan.

Presentation:

These are no beauties - all chunky, caramelly, and uneven. A little confectioners sugar sprinkled lightly on top hides all these faults.

Trust me - you will LOVE these! Luckily they freeze well, so you don't HAVE to eat them at one sitting!

* If you don't cover entire surface, don't worry - it spreads as it bakes.

Uglies

What they lack in looks they make up in personality! These variations of Mandel Brot, Biscotti - whatever, are so delicious that my children insisted that I include them in this book. When you see them, you'll think only a mother could love them. However, when you taste them you'll know why everyone loves them. They are addictive, so BEWARE!

Preheat oven to 350°

In mixer combine and blend on "low":

1 C corn oil
1½ C sugar
4 eggs
4 C flour
2 t baking powder
2 T cinnamon
2 t vanilla

Add and continue blending until incorporated:

2 C chocolate chips
2 C chopped walnuts

Form into 4 long loaves on: ungreased cookie pan

Bake 30 minutes

Cool and slice into 1" - 2" pieces

Turn pieces on side and return to oven for 15 minutes.

Turn over to other side and bake additional 15 minutes.

These Uglies want to be hard, so you may have to adjust baking times.

Now, serve them as is OR:

Melt in double boiler: **1 C chocolate chips**

Dip ½ of each Ugly in melted chocolate and put on parchment paper to harden. You now have: DIPPED UGLIES.

Wonder Truffles

Chopped nuts and chocolate are partners in this large truffle, which is encased in pastry to give you two to three wondrous bites.

Preheat oven to 375°

Pastry:

In mixer, cream until smooth: **2 sticks butter**

Add and mix at "low" until mixture holds together: **½ t vanilla**, **½ C confectioners sugar**, **2 C flour**

Wrap airtight and refrigerate briefly, about one hour.

Truffles:

In food processor finely grind: **1 ²/₃ C almonds**, **1 C chocolate chips**

Add and mix well: **2 egg whites**

Divide into 40 pieces - 1 T each

Roll each into a ball and refrigerate for about one hour.

Now remove refrigerated pastry from refrigerator and break this also into forty pieces.

Dust hands with: **confectioners sugar**

Wrap each pastry around a truffle to cover completely.

Place one inch apart on: cookie sheet, ungreased

Bake 18 minutes.

Presentation:

Sprinkle lightly with: **confectioners sugar**

Coffee Cakes

Apple Breakfast Cake

This is an example of "survival of the fittest". Apple is still the most popular choice - especially if baked in this buttery, rich casserole shape. Johnny Appleseed would be proud!

Preheat oven to 350°

In covered saucepan combine and simmer for 15 minutes:

8 apples, peeled and sliced
2 T sugar
1 T cinnamon
dash nutmeg

In mixer, on "medium" combine:

2 sticks butter
3½ C flour
dash salt
1 T baking powder
1 C sugar
4 eggs
1 T vanilla
¼ C apple juice, from above apples

Mix until well blended.

Pat down with fingers ½ batter onto: 9" x 13" baking pan, greased

Top with: **cooled apple mixture**, drained

Top with: **remaining batter***

In mixer combine:

½ stick butter
½ C brown sugar
¼ C walnuts, chopped

Sprinkle this "streusel" on top of unbaked cake.

Bake 30 - 35 minutes.

Unmold onto clean towel while lukewarm and then invert back right side up onto large platter. To do this, hold towel firmly around cake pan and give a fast flip. Then put serving platter on top of cake (which is now bottom up) and holding edges of towel and bottom of platter, give another fast flip.

Serve warm preferably, but this may be frozen.

Presentation:

Sprinkle lightly with confectioners sugar through a sieve.

Serves 8

*The dough is sticky and will not spread easily. Use hands to make "patties" and lay them over top. If entire top is not covered, don't worry - it spreads together as it bakes.

Apple Cake

So full of healthful apples, the doctor will have to find another profession! A mouthful of cinnamon, raisins, and walnuts - add a cup of coffee or tea and you've achieved perfection!

Prepare apples:

Simmer in covered saucepan for 20 minutes:

4 baking apples, peeled and sliced
½ C sugar
2 t cinnamon
¼ C raisins

Set aside to cool

Heat oven to 350°

Batter:
In mixing bowl, mix on "low":

3 C flour
1½ C sugar
1 C oil
4 eggs
1/3 C apple juice (possibly from above apples)
1 T vanilla
1 heaping T baking powder

Add and mix just until incorporated: **1 C chopped walnuts**

With spatula, drop ½ batter into: 10" teflon lined tube pan, well greased

Follow with: **½ apple mixture**, drained
Follow with: **remaining batter**
Top with: **remaining apple mixture**

Bake 1 hour and 20 - 30 minutes.

Presentation:

Unmold when lukewarm. When cool, sprinkle with confectioners sugar through a sieve.

Serves 12

Apricot Pound Cake

This "comfort" cake has a hint of apricots imbedded in the creamy, satisfying, rich batter. Feeds an army of "not so sweet" lovers. This cake is a MUST MAKE!!

Heat oven to 325°

Combine in mixing bowl and beat on "medium" until fluffy:

2 sticks margarine
1 stick butter
1-8 oz. package cream cheese

Add, and continue to beat: **3 C sugar**

When sugar is incorporated, add and beat in: **6 eggs**

Turn mixer to "low" and add:

3 C flour
1 t baking powder
1 t vanilla

When fully incorporated, turn mixer to "medium" and beat for 10 seconds. Turn off.

With spatula, drop ½ batter into: 10" teflon lined tube pan, well greased

Spoon ring in center of batter with: **4 T thick apricot preserves**

Cover with: remaining batter

Bake 1 hour and 10-20 minutes

When lukewarm, unmold by putting flat dish on top and inverting pan - one palm on top of dish and one palm under cake pan. Turn quickly - it's clumsy but do-able. Now, using same method, invert cake back to upright position onto serving platter

Presentation:

Brush top with: **2 T melted apple jelly**

Make 1-3 daisies with:

dried apricot rounds
8 almond slices, surrounding each round

Make stem and leaves using: **green gel** - comes in small tubes in your grocery baking section

Serves 14-16

Apricot Pound Cake

Blueberry Jam Coffee Cake

This tube shaped confection is the ultimate in coffee cakes. Red wine, jam, fruits, and nuts are contained in each rich slice. This cake slices easily and serves a huge throng. Perfect for a brunch when you entertain your whole neighborhood!

Preheat oven to 350°

In small bowl, soak together:

1 C raisins
1 C sweet blackberry wine

In mixer on "medium," cream until fluffy:

2 sticks butter
1 C sugar

Add:

5 eggs
1 C thick blueberry jam

Turn mixer to "low" and add:

3 1/3 C flour
2 t baking powder
1 t baking soda
dash salt
¾ C buttermilk
raisin-wine mixture*

When well blended, add:

2 C chopped pecans that have been tossed in **2 t flour**

Mix on "medium" for 10 seconds.

Pour into:

10" tube pan, well greased

Bake 1 hour and 10 - 15 minutes.

Unmold when lukewarm

*I'm sorry to say that this step will splash and make a mess in your kitchen. If you have a shield on your mixer, now is a good time to use it, or just have some paper towels handy. It is worth the mess.

Serves 18-20

Chocolate Raspberry Pound Cake

A banquet of raspberries is contained within these chocolate portals of pleasure. If this recipe looks familiar - it is! This is the Apricot Pound Cake with added cocoa and raspberries instead of apricots. Close cousins from a good family!

Preheat oven to 325°

Combine in bowl, beat on "medium" until fluffy:	**2 sticks margarine** **1 stick butter** **1-8 oz. package cream cheese**
Add and continue to beat:	**3 C sugar**
When sugar is incorporated, add and continue to beat:	**6 eggs**
Turn mixer to "low" and add:	**3 C flour** **½ C cocoa** **1 t baking powder** **1 t vanilla**

When fully incorporated, turn mixer to "medium" and beat for 10 seconds. Turn off.

With spatula, drop ½ batter into:	10" teflon lined tube pan, well greased
Spoon "ring" in center of batter with:	**4 T raspberry preserves**
Cover with:	**remaining batter**

Bake 1 hour and 10 - 20 minutes.

When lukewarm, unmold by putting flat dish on top and invert pan - one palm on top of dish and one palm under cake pan. Turn quickly - it's a little clumsy, but do-able. Now invert cake back to right side up on serving platter using same method.

Presentation:

The top of the cake has such a pretty tan, chocolate, mottled look that further embellishment is not necessary. If you must do something - lightly sprinkle top with confectioners sugar and cocoa powder mixture through a strainer.

Serves 14 - 16

Honey Cake

The traditional Jewish New Year cake was always an obligation to eat. This nutty, apple version turns duty into pleasure!

Preheat oven to 350°

Beat on "medium" until creamy:
1 stick butter or margarine
1 C sugar

Add and beat until fluffy:
4 eggs

With mixer on "low" add
1 C honey
1 C apple cider or **juice**
2½ C flour
3 t baking powder
½ t baking soda
1½ t allspice
½ t salt
1 t cinnamon
1 C chopped walnuts
½ C currants
1 apple, unpeeled and grated, seeds removed

Pour into:
2 - 9" x 5" loaf pans, greased
OR
10 C decorative bundt pan, well greased

Bake 40 minutes

Unmold when lukewarm.

Presentation:

When completely cool, dust lightly with confectioners sugar- easy enough?

Each loaf serves 8 - 10

Italian Cornmeal Ring

Buttery, with a hint of tartness. If you like the dry texture of scones, you'll like the feel of this cake. The cornmeal gives a satisfying massage to your mouth. You'll declare, "Mama Mia" - even if you're not Italian!

Preheat oven to 350°

On "medium", beat until fluffy: **2 sticks butter**

Add and beat until creamy: **3½ C confectioners sugar**

Add, and beat until incorporated: **4 eggs**

On "low", add:

2½ C flour
1½ t baking powder
1 C milk
2 T lemon juice
¾ C yellow cornmeal
grated rind from **1 lemon**
pulp from **1 lemon**

Turn to "medium" and beat for 10 seconds.

Scoop into: 10" decorative type bundt pan, well greased

Bake 40 - 50 minutes.

Unmold when lukewarm

Presentation:

Leave as is, or dust a little confectioners sugar on top.

Serves 16-18

Lemon Sponge Cake

Tall and stately, airy, but still moist - is this the best of all possible worlds? When you eat this Passover-appropriate delight, you'll know why this night is different from all other nights!

Preheat oven to 350°

In mixer, beat on "medium" until thick:	**12 egg yolks** **1 T vegetable** or **peanut oil** **1 lemon - juice, pulp** and **grated rind**
Set aside while you work the whites.	
In other bowl, whip on "high" until peaks form:	**12 egg whites**
While slowly sprinkling in:	**1¼ C sugar**
Combine mixtures by hand, using a spatula.	
On top of mixture sprinkle in:	**¾ C matzo cake meal** **¼ C potato starch**

Turn mixer on "low" for 5 - 10 seconds - just until blended. Don't mix too long because you don't want to lose the air from the beaten whites.

Pour into:	10" tube pan with feet, ungreased

Bake 40 - 50 minutes.

When you take the cake out of the oven, invert it onto a platter. In the best of all worlds the cake will slide out in about 4 hours. In real life, you may have to use a thin knife to slide inside the pan perimeter to enable the cake to slide out - either way it's not hard.

Presentation:

Invert the cake onto a platter so that the top is right side up. Sprinkle a little confectioners sugar on the cake. If you have any non-toxic flowers in the house, put one on the bottom - just on one side, with the stem sliding under the cake.

Serves 10 - 12

Plum Kuchen

A seasonal alliance between tart plums and buttery, creamy crust. More a homey than a festive cake.

Preheat oven to 350°

In mixer, on "medium", cream until smooth:	**1 stick butter** **1 C sugar**
Add and continue to mix until incorporated:	**1 C flour** **1 t baking powder** **dash salt** **2 eggs**
Spread mixture into:	8" spring form pan, greased*
Arrange on top of batter:	**6 - 8 halved, pitted, purple plums,** skin side up**
Sprinkle top with:	**½ t sugar** **¼ t cinnamon**

Bake 45 minutes.

Unmold when lukewarm

Serves 6-8

*If you don't have a spring form pan, use a regular round pan, but line the bottom with a parchment paper round. Grease pan and paper round.

**If fresh plums are not available, use a 16 oz. can of well-drained, pitted plums.

Walnut Crown

Crunch, crunch, crunch your way to the stars in this heavenly embodiment of walnuts, butter, and lemon.

Preheat oven to 325°

Turn mixer to "medium" and cream until fluffy:	**2 sticks butter**
Turn mixer to "low" and add:	**1½ C flour** **¾ C sugar** **¼ t baking soda**
When well blended, continue on "low" and add:	grated rind of **1 lemon** **5 egg yolks** **2 t vanilla** **2 T lemon juice**
When well blended, turn off.	
In another bowl, whip on "high":	**5 egg whites**
Slowly adding, until stiff peaks form:	**1 t cream of tartar** **¾ C sugar**
Combine in 1st bowl, using spatula:	**butter-flour batter** **1 C chopped walnuts** **whipped egg whites**

Turn mixture to "low" for 10 seconds. The egg whites and heavier batter should be just mixed and a few white streaks are O.K.

Turn into:	10 C bundt or decorative tube pan, greased

Bake 45 minutes.

Unmold when lukewarm.

Presentation:

Sprinkle a little confectioners sugar through a strainer over top of cake. Surround cake with a "frame" of walnut halves on serving platter.

Serves 8-10

Layer Cakes and Tortes

Banana Cake

You loved this when you were little - and you'll love this now that you're big! Lots of fresh bananas make this a very "homey" and moist cake. The chocolate filling and frosting are incomparable!

Heat oven to 325°

Batter:

In mixer combine, all the while mixing on "low":

2 C flour
1½ C sugar
1 stick margarine
3 ripe bananas, chunked - the browner the better*
¾ C buttermilk
1 t baking soda
1 t baking powder
½ t salt
1 t vanilla

Add and beat on "medium" for 2 minutes: **2 eggs**

Pour batter into: 2 - 9" cake pans, well greased

Bake 25 - 30 minutes.

Unmold when lukewarm

Frosting:

In small double boiler, melt: **¾ C semi-sweet chocolate chips**

In mixing bowl, whip until peaks form: **1½ C whipping cream**

Into whipped cream, swirl in gently with spatula: **chocolate that has slightly cooled**

Presentation:

Spread 1/3 frosting on top of bottom layer. Top with second layer. Using a spatula, spread remaining frosting using an upward motion (as if conducting an orchestra) to get soft peaks on sides and top.

Serves 8

*At last - a way to recycle old bananas: store brown soft bananas in freezer and use them when slightly or completely defrosted.

Carrot Cake

Fresh-grated carrots make this very healthy. Cream cheese and pecans make this very wealthy. Healthy and wealthy - what could be better?

Preheat oven to 325°

Batter:

In mixer, blend on "low" until blended:	**1 $^1/_3$ C vegetable oil** **2 C sugar**
Turn up to "medium", add and beat until fluffy:	**4 eggs**
Turn down to "low", add and mix until blended:	**3 C carrots,** finely grated **2 C flour** **2 t cinnamon** **2 t baking soda**
Turn up to "medium" and beat entire mixture 10 seconds.	
Pour into:	3 - 9" rounds, well greased
Bake 35 - 40 minutes.	

Frosting:

Beat on "medium" until fluffy:	**1-8 oz. package cream cheese** **½ stick butter**
Turn to "low" and add slowly:	**2½ C confectioners sugar**
When sugar is incorporated, add and mix 10 seconds:	**1 $^1/_3$ C pecans,** chopped **1 t vanilla**

Presentation:

Generously frost only tops of layers and stack on top of each other. You will (obviously) have a high three layer cake. If you will not be finishing this within two days, frost sides also to keep the cake moist. Of course, you will spread the tops a little less generously, to accommodate the sides.

At even intervals on top, place:	**3 baby carrots**
Draw in greens with:	**green gel**

Serves 10 - 12

Carrot Cake

Creamy Caramel Cake

This creamy caramel filled delight was originally intended for children's parties - until their parents outran them! This is "comfort" food that takes you back to those days when your needs were simple.

Preheat oven to 350°

Batter:

Combine in mixer, all the while mixing on "low":

1 stick margarine
2 C flour
1 ²/₃ C sugar
1 T baking powder
¼ t baking soda
dash salt
½ C vegetable oil
2 t vanilla
1¼ C buttermilk
3 eggs

Turn mixer to "medium" for 3 minutes

Pour batter into: 2 - 9" rounds, greased

Bake 25-30 minutes.

Unmold when lukewarm.

Filling and Frosting:

Beat in mixer until creamy:

4 oz. cream cheese
2 C confectioners sugar
4 T caramel ice cream topping
4 T heavy cream

Presentation:

Spread filling between layers and on top and sides of cake. If frosting "pulls", thin it with a few drops of heavy cream. Also, if the cake is cold, it will allow the frosting to go on more smoothly.

Press into sides: **1 C butterscotch shards** (p.17)

Serves 8 - 10

Strawberry Mousse Torte

Two hearts that beat as one - soft and feminine yet strong and muscular! The yellow layer is buttery and dense; the filling is creamy and caressing; the frosting is light and fluffy.

Preheat oven to 350°

Batter:

In mixer, on "medium", beat until smooth: **2 sticks butter**
1¼ C confectioners sugar

Add: **3 eggs**

Turn mixer to "low" and add: **1½ C flour**
2 t strawberry jam

Mix for 20 seconds.
Spread into: 9" springform pan, greased

Bake 45 minutes.

Unmold when lukewarm, and when cool, split into two layers using a serrated knife, with a sawing motion.

Filling:

Beat on "medium" until smooth: **4 oz. cream cheese**
2 T confectioners sugar
½ C drained frozen strawberries, packed in heavy syrup

In separate bowl whip until peaks form: **¼ C whipping cream**

Combine both mixtures

Spread this on bottom layer that you split. Cover with top layer.

Frosting:

In mixer on "medium" beat until smooth: **2 sticks butter**
1 C confectioners sugar

Add: **½ can sweetened condensed milk** (cans come in 14 oz. size)
1 t vanilla
½ C frozen strawberries, drained

Beat until well mixed.

Presentation:

Spread frosting generously on top and sides of cake. With spoon make half circles - the frosting is dense enough to retain the shapes.
Serves 10

Variations that you can use on this cake:

1. You may omit the top frosting and cover the top cake layer with fresh strawberries arranged in a pretty design (shown on this page.)
2. You may make the frosting and leave out the frozen strawberries - leaving you with a wonderful buttercream. Then you will have a creamy white colored cake.
3. You may use the above white buttercream and then arrange with fresh strawberries.
4. You decide what to do - I can't do all the work around here!

White Forest Torte

In this Strauss waltz, whipping cream and cherries join hands and perform gracefully. Eat a piece and you will be transported to the forests of Bavaria.

Preheat oven to 350°

Batter:

In mixer, whip until very soft peaks form:	**1½ C whipping cream**
Add and continue to beat on "medium":	**3 eggs** **1 t almond extract**
Turn off mixer. With spatula, mixing by hand, add:	**2 C flour** **1½ C sugar** **2 t baking powder** **dash salt**

Turn mixer to "low" for 10 seconds - or until just incorporated.

Pour batter into:	2 - 9" pans, greased

Bake 20-25 min.

Unmold when lukewarm.

Filling:

Combine in bowl:	**1 C thick cherry preserves** **2 T Amaretto liqueur**

Frosting:

In mixer, whip until peaks form:	**1 C whipping cream** **½ C confectioners sugar** **1 t vanilla**

Presentation:

Spread bottom layer with:	**cherry preserve filling**
Put 2nd layer on top and frost top and sides with:	**whipped cream frosting**
With a spoon, swirl around to create a marbled effect:	**1 t cherry preserves**
Press into sides:	**1 C white chocolate shards** (p.17)

Serves 10

Nut Cakes and Tortes

Feud Cake

This authentic southern recipe substitutes finely ground pecans for almost every other ingredient. The subtle flavor of pecans is enhanced by a fresh whipped cream filling and frosting. A true southern beauty!

Preheat oven to 350°

Batter:

In mixer, beat on "medium" until thick:

6 egg yolks
1½ C sugar

On "low", add just until blended:

3 T flour
1 t baking powder
3 C pecans, ground

In other bowl, whip on high until peaks form:

6 egg whites

Combine both mixtures on "low" for 5 seconds - just until blended.

Pour batter into:

2 - 8" cake pans, well greased

Bake 25 minutes.

Unmold when lukewarm.

Filling & Frosting:

Beat until peaks form:

2 C whipping cream
6 T confectioners sugar
1 t vanilla

Presentation:

Spread frosting thickly between layers. Spread top and sides of cake as if you were conducting an orchestra - that way you will get soft peaks all around. Don't worry if you're not musically inclined - if you can't get pretty peaks, sprinkle top and sides with:

pecans, coarsely chopped

Surround cake on platter with:

pecan halves forming a frame

Serves 8

Hazelnut Coffee Roulade

A duet of hazelnuts and coffee sing this sweet ballad of moist crunchiness. Aside from all this flowery gibberish, this cake is GREAT!

Preheat oven to 350°

Batter:

In bowl, beat on "medium" until thick and lemon colored: **5 egg yolks**, **½ C sugar**

Add, with mixer on "low": **1 t coffee**, cooled; **1¼ C hazelnuts (filberts),** ground*; **2 T flour**; **¾ t baking powder**

In other bowl, whip: **5 egg whites**

Slowly add until peaks form: **pinch, cream of tartar**; **¼ C sugar**

Add whites to yolk mixture and mix on "low" 15 seconds.

Pour batter onto: 10" x 15" jelly roll pan, greased, cover with parchment paper, greased

Bake 15-20 minutes.

Filling:

In small saucepan, on low heat, dissolve: **1 t instant coffee**, **1 t water**

Add: **6 T sweetened condensed milk**

Heat until thermometer registers 160°, then cool

In mixer, whip until peaks form: **¾ C whipping cream**

Add to whipped cream, and mix on "low" for 10 seconds: **coffee, sweet milk mixture**; **¼ C hazelnuts,** ground

Presentation:

Spread filling on cooled cake.
Using parchment as "lifter", roll from wide side into a jelly roll, creating a long roll.
Tuck parchment tightly around roll to keep its shape and refrigerate or freeze for one hour.
Place on long platter and surround with fern fronds or lemon leaves. Simple and elegant!

Serves 8-10

*If your hazelnuts have the brown, papery membrane, do this: Heat nuts at 350° for about 5 minutes. Remove from oven and put onto kitchen towel. Rub all around nuts and uncover. The membrane will have fallen off most of the nuts. Now proceed with recipe.

Nusstorte

This nut cake is so authentically Viennese, that if it could, it would waltz to your plate! Finely chopped walnuts are the main ingredients of this slightly lemony delight. The frosting is a chocolate fudge dream.

Preheat oven to 325°

Batter:

Beat on "medium" until thick:
4 egg yolks
¾ C sugar

Add and blend on "low" 2 minutes:
3 T breadcrumbs
½ lemon - juice, pulp, grated rind
1 t baking powder
1 C walnuts - ground to tiny chunks - not too fine.

In other bowl, whip until peaks form:
4 egg whites

Fold whites into nut mixture and blend on "low" for 10 seconds.

Pour into:
9" round or spring form pan, well greased

Bake 35-40 minutes.

Unmold when lukewarm.

Frosting:

Combine in mixer, and beat until smooth:
1 stick butter
¼ C confectioners sugar
2 T unsweetened cocoa
1 T rum

Presentation:

Spread frosting on top and sides of cake.

Make ring of walnut halves on top.

Touch up each walnut with 2-3 "leaves" made with:
green gel

Serves 10-12

Viennese Almond Kahlua Torte

Yo, ho, ho and a bottle of Kahlua! Ground almonds and chocolate too!

Preheat oven to 375°

Batter:

In mixer, beat on "medium" until smooth:	**1 stick butter** **¾ C sugar**
With mixer on, add:	**6 egg yolks** **2 T Kahlua** **½ C chocolate chips**, grated **1 ⅔ C almonds,** grated **¼ C** and **1 T bread crumbs** **1 T baking powder**
In separate bowl, whip until peaks form:	**6 egg whites** **¼ C sugar** **dash salt**

Fold egg whites into chocolate-nut mixture. Blend on "low" for 10 seconds.

Pour into:	9" spring form pan, greased, lined with parchment circle, greased parchment

Bake 40-50 minutes.
Unmold when lukewarm and peel off parchment.

Frosting:

In mixer, beat until smooth:	**1 stick butter** **½ C chocolate chips**, melted **2 T confectioners sugar** **2 T cocoa** **1 T Kahlua**

Presentation:

Frost top and sides with frosting.

Make "daisy" on top by sticking into cake:	**1 almond**, point sticking up
Surround almond point with petals made of:	**8 almond slices**

Serves 10

Almond “Daisy”

whole almond
stuck into cake
pointy side down

sliced almonds

Variety Cakes

Lemon Crunch Roll

Yellow genoise rolls around tart lemon curd. Perfect partnership between "puckery" and "crunchy"! If you love lemon, you will love this cake; if you just like lemon, you will still love this cake.

Lemon Curd Filling: Best made 1 day ahead and refrigerated:

In heavy saucepan, combine:	**2 eggs** **2 egg yolks** **½ C sugar** **2 lemons, juice & pulp** **1 stick butter**, cut up

Turn heat to "low", stir constantly until thermometer registers 160°.

Stir in:	**rind** from **2 lemons**
When cold, stir in:	**¼ C white chocolate,** chopped

Refrigerate at least 8 hours.

Preheat oven to 425°

Genoise (sponge roll):

In mixer, beat on "medium" until thick:	**2 eggs** **2 egg yolks** **½ C sugar**
When thick, add:	**1 t vanilla**
In other bowl, whip until peaks form:	**2 egg whites** **1 T sugar**
Add egg whites to egg yolks and sprinkle on top:	**½ C flour**

Turn mixer to "low" and mix for 10 seconds.

Spread mixture onto:	10" x 15" jelly roll pan, greased parchment paper, greased

Bake 5 - 8 minutes

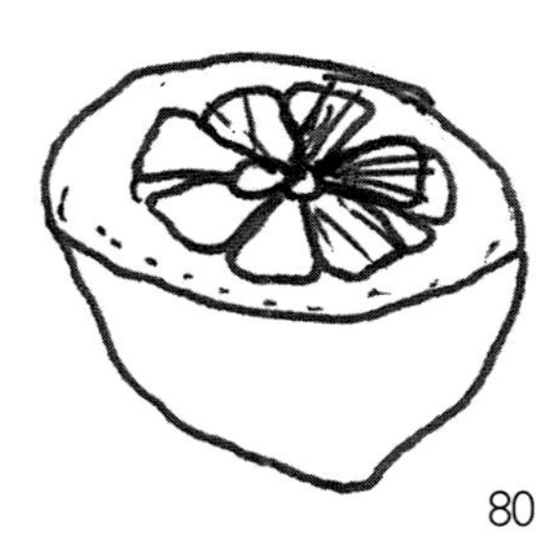

Presentation:

When cool, lift genoise from pan by lifting parchment paper sides. Spread most of lemon curd on roll - reserving about 2 T for topping.

Using parchment as handle, roll short side into jelly roll - resulting in a fat, short roll*

Place this in freezer for short time to set filling in place and keep shape of roll together.

Frosting

Whip in mixer until peaks form:

½ C whipping cream
2 t confectioners sugar

Spread whipping cream on cold roll. Use reserved lemon curd to swirl on top and sides to get a subtle lemon marbled effect.

Sprinkle top with:

¼ C white chocolate, chopped

Serves 6-8

*This may also be made as a three layer loaf. Cut frosted cake into three strips at width. Pile on top of each other and frost as above.

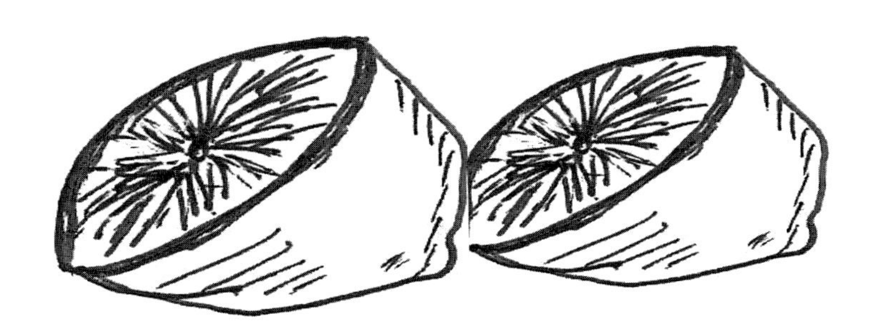

Lemon Crunch Roll

Pumpkin Nut Roll

Slightly spicy pumpkin roll encases a creamy maple filling. Outside is studded with nuts. This Thanksgiving treat is the real reason that the Pilgrims came to the New World.

Preheat oven to 350°

Batter:

In mixer, on "medium", beat until thick:

3 eggs
1 C sugar

Turn to "low" and add:

2/3 C canned pumpkin*
1 t lemon juice
¾ C flour
1 t baking powder
2 t cinnamon
1 t ginger
½ t nutmeg

Turn off mixer when just well blended.

Pour into:

15" x 10" jelly roll pan, greased, parchment lined, greased

Sprinkle with:

1 C walnuts or **hazelnuts,** chopped

Bake 12 minutes.

When lukewarm, unmold onto clean kitchen towel. Peel off parchment. Nut side is on bottom.

Filling:

Cream:

1- 8 oz. package cream cheese
4 T butter

Add:

1 C confectioners sugar
4 t maple syrup

In separate bowl, whip until peaks form:

½ C whipping cream

Combine ingredients from both bowls and mix on "low" for 5 seconds.

Presentation:

Spread filling evenly on surface of "un"-nutted side.
Using towel as "pusher", roll from short narrow end - thereby making a fat, high roll.

Using towel, tighten ends, so that roll stays compact and firm, and put in freezer for a short while before serving.

The nuts look so pretty that further embellishment is not necessary. Of course, a few greens surrounding roll always make for an elegant presentation.

Serves 10

* Be sure to buy plain canned pumpkin - not pumpkin pie mixture.

The Bakers' Magic

Add flour, sugar, milk, and eggs,
chocolate, lemon, or whatever flavor
your heart desires; your taste buds crave.
Add them together, in one large bowl, and stir.
Can you now separate even one ingredient?
No! Why ever would you consider such a move?

Now, you bake and wait, wait, wait,
for the magic to take shape, the aroma, the taste,
the sweet memories, and dreams,
future memories, of today's encounter,
with this token of a baker's love.

Can you now separate one element, of this miracle,
coming from generation to generation,
mother to daughter, to grandchild?
Recipes handed down by word of mouth,
words in books, from land to land, age to age,
until, finally, in your eager hands,
the steps are repeated, along with your special affection,
that will make this gift of love continue,
through the ages, by the magic, of the baker's oven.

Stuart I. Opperer

Notes

Index

See order form- reverse side

Order Form

Name____

Address______________________________________

City ________________ **State** ______________ **Zip**________

Telephone____________________________________

Additional addresses to send as gifts:

Name____

Address______________________________________

City ________________ **State** ______________ **Zip**________

Telephone____________________________________

Note enclosure to say____________________________

Please send_______ copies of "Desserts - A Delicious Learning, Baking, and Eating Experience"

Price per book	**$19.95 x ____ =__________**
Tax per book	**$ 1.20 x ____ =__________**
Shipping per book	**$ 3.25 x ____ =__________**
Total	**$__________**

Make check payable to Green Tree Publishing, LLC

MAIL TO: **GREEN TREE PUBLISHING, LLC**
P.O. BOX 205
BIRMINGHAM, MI 48012-0205

THANK YOU FOR YOUR ORDER, AND ENJOY THE BOOK.

Sylvia